Cheesecake Bars Made Easy

Delicious Cheesecake Bars Recipes to Make You Swoon

Table of Contents

Introduction *4*

Recipe 1. Ginger Lemon Cheesecake Bars......................7

Recipe 2. Strawberry Cheesecake Cookie Bars..............9

Recipe 3. Baklava Cheesecake Bars 11

Recipe 4. Cheesecake Brownies 14

Recipe 5. Rainbow Vanilla Cheesecake Bars...............16

Recipe 6. Blueberry Cheesecake Bars 19

Recipe 7. Sopapilla Cheesecake Bars 21

Recipe 8. Red Velvet Cheesecake Bars 23

Recipe 9. Lemon Blueberry Cheesecake Bites.............26

Recipe 10. Black and Orange Cheesecake Bars 28

Recipe 11. Cheesecake Lemon Bars............................31

Recipe 12. Coconut Cheesecake Bars 34

Recipe 13. Chocolate Chip Cheesecake Bars 37

Recipe 14. Nutella Swirl Cheesecake Bars..................41

Recipe 15. Pumpkin Cheesecake Streusel Bars............43

Recipe 16. Chocolate Mint Cheesecake Bars 46

Recipe 17. Vanilla Bean Cheesecake Bars 49

Recipe 18. Key Lime Pie Cheesecake Bars....................52

Recipe 19. Red Velvet Cheesecake Swirl Brownies 55

Recipe 20. Strawberry Margarita Cheesecake Bars 58

Recipe 21. Caramel Cheesecake Bars 61

Recipe 22. Toaster Strudel Cheesecake Bars 64

Recipe 23. New York Cheesecake Bars 67

Recipe 24. Peanut Butter and Jelly Cheesecake Bars....69

Recipe 25. Cranberry Almond Cheesecake Bars...........72

Recipe 26. Caramel Pecan Cheesecake Bars.................75

Recipe 27. Cranberry Almond Cheesecake Bars...........78

Recipe 28. Simple Cheesecake Bars.............................81

Recipe 29. Pineapple Cheesecake Bars 83

Recipe 30. Eggnog Cheesecake Bars............................87

Introduction

You find yourself craving some cheesecake bars, but you can't make them from scratch.

Cream cheese is expensive, and none of your recipes turn out like a true cheesecake bar.

Let the Cheesecake Bars Made Easy book take care of the baking for you.

There are so many desserts that exist in the world, but nothing beats a cheesecake bar. It doesn't matter how old you are, where you're from, or if you're a man or a woman. The cheesecake bar is the perfect dessert for everyone. With its light, sweet, and creamy taste, it's the perfect treat to satisfy your sweet tooth.

Cheesecake Bars Made Easy is the perfect book for anyone who wants to make delicious cheesecake bars without any fuss. Created by a professional cheesecake baker, this book contains 30 recipes that will have you licking your lips in no time. From classic cheesecake bars to variations like Red Velvet Cheesecake Swirl Brownies, there's something for everyone in this book.

Features:

30 delicious cheesecake bars recipes

A variety of flavors to choose from

Images, instructions, and ingredients for each recipe

Easy to make - even for those who are not experienced bakers

A fun and easy way to get your friends and family involved in the kitchen

Perfect for any occasion, from small get-togethers to large parties

We know that not everyone has the time or energy to spend hours in the kitchen cooking up a delicious cheesecake. That's why our Cheesecake Bars Made Easy recipe book is perfect for those of you who want an easy, foolproof way to enjoy cheesecake without all the fuss. Simply follow the recipes in this book and you'll be enjoying delicious cheesecake bars in no time at all!

So, what are you waiting for? Start cooking today with this easy-to-use book!

Recipe 1. Ginger Lemon Cheesecake Bars

Preparation time-25 minutes

Servings –18

The List of Ingredients:

Crust:

1. ½ ounce ground ginger
2. 2 ounces melted butter
3. 16 ounces crushed gingersnaps
4. 2 ½ ounces brown sugar

Cheesecake:

1. 2 ounces lemon juice
2. 2 eggs
3. 1/3 ounce lemon extract
4. 4 ounces white sugar
5. 16 ounces softened cream cheese

Method:

Step 1   Preheat oven to 350 degrees Fahrenheit

Step 2   Mix brown sugar, butter, gingersnaps, ginger, and butter in a large bowl

Step 3   Press the gingersnap mixture along the bottom of a baking dish (9"x13") to create a crust

Step 4   Bake for 8 minutes, then remove from heat and cool

Step 5   Blend the rest of the Ingredients in a food processor until smooth and spread evenly over the cookie crust

Step 6   Bake for 30 minutes or until firm

Step 7   Remove from heat and let the cheesecake cool to room temperature, then chill for 1 ½ hours before serving

Recipe 2. Strawberry Cheesecake Cookie Bars

Preparation time-20 minutes

Servings –18

The List of Ingredients:

1. 24 ounces softened cream cheese

2. 4 ounces seedless strawberry jam

3. 16 ½ ounces refrigerated sugar cookie dough

4. 4 ounces sugar

5. 3 large eggs

Method:

Step 1   Preheat oven to 350 degrees Fahrenheit

Step 2   Roll cookie dough along the bottom of a baking pan (9"x13") and press down to create an even layer

Step 3   Beat cream cheese and sugar in a bowl with an electric mixer until smooth

Step 4   Beat eggs into the cream cheese one at a time, making sure each is blended before adding the next

Step 5   Pour cream cheese filling over the dough in the baking pan

Step 6   Pour jam into an icing bag or Ziploc bag and pipe jam over the cream cheese in five thick lines along the length of the baking pan.

Step 7   Drag a skewer through the jam lines to create patterns

Step 8   Bake for 1 hour or until set, then remove from heat and cool for 30 minutes

Step 9   Chill for 2 hours before cutting into 18 bars and serving

Recipe 3. Baklava Cheesecake Bars

Preparation time-30 minutes

Servings –36

The List of Ingredients:

1. 12 ounces sugar

2. ½ teaspoon cinnamon, ground

3. ½ teaspoon lemon zest

4. 16 ounces refrigerated crescent dough sheet

5. 2 ounces honey

6. 1 teaspoon freshly squeezed lemon juice

7. 16 ounces finely chopped walnuts

8. 16 ounces softened cream cheese

Method:

Step 1   Preheat oven to 350 degrees Fahrenheit

Step 2   Roll out 1 can of dough along the bottom of a baking dish (9"x13"), pressing down to create one even layer of dough

Step 3   Beat cream cheese, 8 ounces sugar and the lemon zest with an electric mixer in a large bowl until smooth

Step 4   Spread the cream cheese over the dough in the baking dish

Step 5   In another bowl, mix 4 ounces of sugar, cinnamon and walnuts until well combined and sprinkle this mixture over the cream cheese

Step 6   Unroll the other can of dough on a flat surface and carefully place over the top layer in the baking dish. Gently stretch the dough to cover the whole baking dish

Step 7   Mix lemon juice and honey and brush over the dough

Step 8   Bake for 35 minutes or until golden brown

Step 9   Remove from heat and cool for 30 minutes, then

            chill for 4 hours

Step 10   Cut into bars before serving

Recipe 4. Cheesecake Brownies

Preparation time-15 minutes

Servings –24

The List of Ingredients:

1. 20 ounces packaged brownie mix
2. 8 ounces softened cream cheese
3. 1 large egg
4. 2 ½ ounces white sugar

Method:

Step 1   Prepare brownie mix according to package

Step 2   Coat a baking pan (9"x13") with cooking spray

Step 3   Pour the brownie batter into the pan

Step 4   Beat the rest of the Ingredients with an electric mixture until smooth then spread the cream cheese evenly over the brownie batter in the pan

Step 5   Swirl with a skewer to create designs

Step 6   Bake according to Method: on the brownie package. Remove from heat and cool until the brownies are room temperature, then cut into bars before serving

Recipe 5. Rainbow Vanilla Cheesecake Bars

Preparation time-20 minutes

Servings –24

The List of Ingredients:

1. 24 ounces softened cream cheese

2. 30 crushed Golden Oreo cookies

3. 1 drop of the following gel food colors; red, orange, green, yellow, blue and violet (use more for desired shade)

4. 14 ounces white sugar

5. 1 1/3 teaspoons vanilla extract

6. cooking spray

7. 3 large eggs

8. 1 ½ ounces sour cream

9. 1 ½ ounces all-purpose flour

Method:

Step 1   Preheat the oven to 325 degrees Fahrenheit

Step 2   Coat a baking pan (9"x13") with cooking spray

Step 3   Form a crust with the cookies by pressing them into the bottom of the baking pan in one even layer

Step 4   Using an electric mixer, beat the cream cheese and sugar together until smooth

Step 5   Add eggs, flour, sour cream and vanilla to the cream cheese and beat until well combined

Step 6   Spread half of the cream cheese batter over the crust in the baking pan

Step 7   Split the rest of the cream cheese mixture evenly between 6 small bowls and add a different color food coloring to teach bowl. Add more drops to get desired shades

Step 8   Add the colors to the top of the white batter in the
           baking pan in a random order and use skewers to
           swirl the colors together

Step 9   Bake for 45 minutes or until just set in the
           middle. Remove from heat and let cool for 2-3
           hours to room temperature. Cover the top with
           wrap and chill for 4-6 hours

Step 10   Cut into squares before serving

Recipe 6. Blueberry Cheesecake Bars

Preparation time-20 minutes

Servings –24

The List of Ingredients:

1. 1 teaspoon vanilla

2. 2 large eggs

3. 3 ounces melted butter

4. 16 ounces softened cream cheese

5. 6 ounces sugar

6. 10 ounces of blueberry preserves

7. 16 ounces crushed graham cracker

8. 8 ounces blueberries

Method:

Step 1   Preheat oven to 350 degrees Fahrenheit

Step 2   Combine butter and graham cracker crumbs and form a crust by pressing into the bottom of a baking pan (9"x13")

Step 3   Beat cream cheese and sugar in a bowl with an electric mixer until smooth. Then beat in eggs and vanilla until combined well

Step 4   Stir the preserves while in the jar so it softens, then spread on the graham cracker crust. Layer the berries over the jam and pour the cream cheese over the berries.

Step 5   Bake for 30 minutes or until slightly puffy. Remove from heat and let the cheesecake cool. Cut into bars and serve.

Recipe 7. Sopapilla Cheesecake Bars

Preparation time-15 minutes

Servings –20

The List of Ingredients:

1. 16 ounces softened cream cheese
2. 4 ounces melted butter
3. 16 ounces refrigerated crescent dinner rolls
4. ½ ounce cinnamon, ground
5. 12 ounces sugar
6. 1teaspoon vanilla

Method:

Step 1   Preheat oven to 350 degrees F

Step 2   Roll 8 ounce can of dough along the bottom of a baking dish (9"x13") and press down to make an even layer

Step 3   Beat cream cheese and 8 ounces of sugar in a bowl with an electric mixer until smooth

Step 4   Add vanilla and beat until well combined

Step 5   Spread cream cheese mixture on the dough in the baking dish

Step 6   Unroll the other 8 ounce can of crescent roll dough and gently place on the cream cheese in the baking pan. Pinch the seams of the dough together to create a single solid sheet

Step 7   Pour butter over the top of the dough evenly.

Step 8   Combine 4 ounces of sugar and cinnamon and sprinkle the mixture over the butter

Step 9   Bake for 30 minutes or until set

Step 10   Remove from heat and let the cheesecake cool to room temperature

Step 11   Chill for 1-2 hours

Recipe 8. Red Velvet Cheesecake Bars

Preparation time-20 minutes

Servings –24

The List of Ingredients:

Crust:

1. 17 ½ ounces of double chocolate cookie mix

2. ¼ teaspoon red food coloring

3. 1 large egg

4. 4 ounces butter

Cheesecake:

1. 4 ounces butter
2. 1 ounce all-purpose flour
3. 3 large eggs
4. 4 ounces heavy whipping cream
5. 12 ounces white sugar
6. 1/3 ounce vanilla extract
7. 16 ounces softened cream cheese

Topping:

1. 8 ounces milk chocolate chips

Method:

Step 1   Preheat the oven to 400 degrees Fahrenheit

Step 2   Grease a baking pan (9"x13") with butter

Step 3   Combine 4 ounces of butter, cookie mix, 1 egg and red food coloring in a bowl and stir thoroughly

Step 4   Transfer mixture to the pan and spread it out into an even layer along the bottom

Step 5   Using an electric mixer, beat cream cheese, 4 ounces of butter, sugar and 3 eggs in a large bowl on medium high

Step 6   Gradually add flour, cream and vanilla and beat for 2 minutes until smooth. Scrape the sides of the bowl as you go.

Step 7   Pour the cheesecake mixture over the cookie dough in the pan and bake for 45 minutes or until set.

Step 8   Remove from heat and let the cheesecake cool

Step 9   In 15-30 second intervals, melt chocolate in a microwaveable bowl until smooth. Stir after every interval.

Step 10   Spread the chocolate over the cheesecake and cover with wrap

Step 11   Chill for 4 hours, then cut into bars and serve

Recipe 9. Lemon Blueberry Cheesecake Bites

Preparation time-5 minutes

Servings –2

The List of Ingredients:

1. 12 fresh blueberries
2. 2 Fiber One lemon bars, cut diagonally
3. 1 ounce softened cream cheese
4. ½ teaspoon confectioners' sugar

Method:

Step 1   Beat cream cheese and sugar in a bowl with an electric mixer until smooth

Step 2   Place the lemon bars on a flat dish and spread the cream cheese evenly over each

Step 3   Top with blueberries and sugar

Recipe 10. Black and Orange Cheesecake Bars

Preparation time-20 minutes

Servings –25

The List of Ingredients:

1. 1 ½ ounces all-purpose flour

2. 1 ½ ounces melted butter

3. 12 ounces crushed Oreo cookies

4. 24 ounces softened cream cheese

5. 1 teaspoon vanilla

6. ½ ounce whipping cream

7. 3 eggs

8. 1/3 ounces orange zest

9. 2 ounces chopped baking chocolate, semisweet

10. 6 ounces sugar

11. 1 teaspoon orange food coloring

Method:

Step 1   Preheat oven to 325 degrees Fahrenheit

Step 2   Line a square baking pan (9"x9") with enough aluminum foil to allow some of it to hang over the edges of the pan. Coat the foil with a light layer of cooking spray

Step 3   Mix cookies and butter in a bowl until well combined, then press the cookie mixture into the bottom of the baking pan so you form an even layer of crust that covers the whole surface

Step 4   Bake for 10 minutes, remove from heat and let cool to room temperature

Step 5   While crust is cooling, beat cream cheese and sugar in a bowl with an electric mixer until smooth

Step 6   Add orange zest, flour, vanilla and food coloring to the cream cheese and beat until completely blended together. Beat eggs into the batter one at a time, combining completely before adding the next

Step 7   Pour the cream cheese over the crust in the baking pan

Step 8   Bake for 45 minutes or until set, then remove from oven and let the cheesecake cool for 1 hour. Chill for 2-4 hours

Step 9   Microwave chocolate and whipped topping on high in 15 second increments and stir at each interval until they are completely melted

Step 10   Drizzle chocolate over the chilled cheesecake and use the foil to lift the cake onto a serving dish. Cut into bars and serve.

Recipe 11. Cheesecake Lemon Bars

Preparation time-30 minutes

Servings –24

The List of Ingredients:

1. 4 ounces lemon juice
2. 12 ounces white sugar
3. 6 ounces butter, cut into cubes
4. ½ ounce all-purpose flour
5. 4 large eggs
6. 16 ounces softened cream cheese

7. 12 ounces all-purpose flour

8. 4 ounces confectioners' sugar

9. ½ ounce lemon zest

10. 2 beaten eggs

11. 8 ounces white sugar

Method:

Step 1   Preheat an oven to 350 degrees Fahrenheit

Step 2   Lightly grease a baking dish(9"x13") with butter

Step 3   Whisk 12 ounces of flour and confectioners' sugar in a bowl. Add butter to the flour mixture and cut it until it looks like coarse meal

Step 4   Form a crust in the baking pan by pressing the flour mix into the bottom of the baking pan in one even layer

Step 5   Bake for 18 minutes or until golden brown. Remove from heat and let it cool to room temperature

Step 6   Whisk 12 ounces of sugar, 4 eggs, ½ ounce of flour, lemon zest and juice in a bowl

Step 7   Pour the sugar and lemon mixture into the crust. Smooth the surface by removing bubbles.

Step 8   Mix cream cheese and 8 ounces of sugar in a bowl with an electric mixer until smooth

Step 9   Whisk in 2 eggs to the cream cheese and spread
           this over the lemon in the baking pan

Step 10   Bake for 30 minutes or until set

Recipe 12. Coconut Cheesecake Bars

Preparation time-10 minutes

Servings –12

The List of Ingredients:

Crust:

1. 4 ounces sugar
2. 6 ½ ounces package GOYA Chocolate Maria Cookies
3. 5 ounces melted butter, unsalted

Cheesecake:

1. 16 ounces softened cream cheese

2. 15 ounces canned cream of coconut, stirred

3. 1/8 teaspoon salt

4. 2 large eggs

5. 1/2 teaspoon vanilla extract

6. 24 ounces sweetened coconut, shredded

Method:

Step 1   Heat oven to 350 degrees Fahrenheit

Step 2   Line a cake pan (9"x13") with a large piece of aluminum foil so that some of the foil hangs over the edge

Step 3   Coat the lined pan with butter and set aside

Step 4   Place cookies and sugar in a blender and pulse until the mixture turns into crumbs, then add the butter and pulse for 30 seconds

Step 5   Spread crumbs along the bottom of the baking pan and press down to form an even crust

Step 6   Bake for 15 minutes, removed from heat and set aside until it reaches room temperature

Step 7   Beat cream cheese, coconut cream and salt with an electric mixer on medium high for 4 minutes

Step 8   Change the speed of the mixer to low and beat the eggs into the mixture one at a time until well combined, while also adding vanilla.

Step 9   Transfer cream cheese mix to the baking pan and top with coconut

Step 10   Bake for 45 minutes or until edges are puffy but the cake is not quite set

Step 11   Remove from heat and let cool to room temperature, then chill for 4 hours

Step 12   Lift the cheesecake from the pan using the tin foil and cut into squares

Recipe 13. Chocolate Chip Cheesecake Bars

Preparation time-20 minutes

Servings –16

The List of Ingredients:

Cookie

1. 1 teaspoon vanilla extract

2. 6 ounces softened butter

3. 5 ½ ounces granulated sugar

4. ¾ teaspoon salt

5. 1 egg yolk

6. 1 ½ teaspoons cornstarch

7. 1 whole egg

8. 16 ounces all-purpose flour

9. 8 ounces milk chocolate chips

10. ½ teaspoon baking powder

11. 6 ounces firmly packed brown sugar

Cheesecake

1. ¾ teaspoon vanilla extract

2. 2 eggs

3. ⅓ cup sour cream

4. 5 ½ ounces granulated sugar

5. 24 ounces softened cream cheese

Method:

Step 1   Preheat oven to 350 degrees Fahrenheit

Step 2   Line a baking pan (11"x7") with aluminum foil
            and coat the foil with cooking spray

Cookie layer:

Step 1   Beat the butter and sugar together using an
            electric mixer until fluffy

Step 2   Stir in egg and egg yolk until thoroughly combined

Step 3   Add vanilla extract and stir well

Step 4   Whisk flour, cornstarch, salt and baking powder in another bowl until well combined

Step 5   Add slowly the flour mixture to the egg and stir until the dry mixture is completely combined with the wet. Add chocolate chips to the batter and stir well.

Step 6   Form a layer along the bottom of the baking pan by pouring half of the batter along the bottom and pressing down to even it out

Step 7   Set the other half of the cookie batter aside

Cheesecake layer:

Step 1   Beat cream cheese and sugar together with a mixer in a large bowl until smooth and you use peaks forming

Step 2   Add vanilla and stir until well combined. Do the same with the sour cream.

Step 3   Gradually stir in sour cream until combined.

Step 4   Pour cheesecake filling over the cookie layer in the baking pan

Step 5   Randomly drop the rest of the cookie drop in spoonfuls over the cheesecake layer

Step 6   Bake for 35 minutes or until the top layer turns golden brown and the cheesecake is set

Step 7   Remove from heat and cool until it reaches room temperature. Chill for 6-8 hours, then cut it into bars and serve

Recipe 14. Nutella Swirl Cheesecake Bars

Preparation time-20 minutes

Servings –32

The List of Ingredients:

1. 4 ounces sugar

2. 2 ½ ounces Nutella

3. 16 ounces softened cream cheese

4. 16 ounces refrigerated chocolate chip cookies dough

5. 2 large eggs

6.   1 teaspoon vanilla

Method:

Step 1   Preheat the oven to 350 degrees Fahrenheit

Step 2   Roll dough along the bottom of a baking pan (9"x13") and press down to create one even layer

Step 3   Bake for 13 mins or until golden brown. Remove from heat and cool while you work on the filling

Step 4   Beat cream cheese, vanilla and sugar with an electric mixer in a large bowl. Add eggs one at time and beat before adding the next one

Step 5   Spread the cream cheese over the crust in the baking pan

Step 6   In a microwave-safe bowl, melt Nutella in 10 second intervals, stirring until melted

Step 7   Drop small amounts of Nutella into the cream cheese and swirl it around with a skewer to create a pattern

Step 8   Bake for 30 minutes or until set

Step 9   Remove from heat and let the cheesecake cool for 30 minutes, then chill for 2-4 hours

Step 10   Cut into 32 bars and serve

Recipe 15. Pumpkin Cheesecake Streusel Bars

Preparation time-20 minutes

Servings –24

The List of Ingredients:

1. 1 ½ teaspoons pumpkin pie spice

2. ½ cup quick-cooking oats

3. 15 ounces canned pumpkin

4. 6 ounces sugar

5. 8 ounces softened cream cheese

6. 1 ½ rolls Pillsbury™ chocolate chip cookies (24.75 oz, refrigerated)

7. 3 eggs

Method:

Step 1   Preheat oven to 350 degrees Fahrenheit

Step 2   Line a baking pan (9"x13") with aluminum foil and coat the foil with a light layer of cooking spray

Step 3   Roll 16 ½ ounces or 1 roll of cookie dough along the bottom of the baking pan and press down to create one even layer

Step 4   Bake for 10 minutes and remove from heat and let cool while you make the cheesecake

Step 5   Crumble ½ a roll (8 ounces) of cookie dough in a bowl with your fingers and mix in 4 ounce s of oats into the dough until you get a crumbly consistency

Step 6   In a separate bowl, beat 15 ounces of pumpkin, 3 eggs, 8 ounces cream cheese, 6 ounces of sugar and 1 ½ teaspoons of pumpkin spice with an electric mixer until smooth and lump-free.

Step 7   Pour pumpkin over the crust in the baking pan

and sprinkle the cookie dough and oats streusel over top evenly

Step 8   Bake for 30 minutes or until just set in the center

Step 9   Turn the heat off in the oven and let the cheesecake sit on the rack for 45 minutes. Place in the refrigerator to chill for 2-4 hours, then cut into 24 bars and serve.

Recipe 16. Chocolate Mint Cheesecake Bars

Preparation time-20 minutes

Servings –24

The List of Ingredients:

1. 16 ounces cream cheese frosting

2. 4 ounces softened butter

3. 10 ounces dark chocolate and mint chips

4. 3 large eggs

5. 24 ounces softened cream cheese

6. 6 drops green food coloring

7. 18 ¼ ounces chocolate fudge cake mix with pudding

8. 3 drops creme de menthe candy flavoring

Method:

Step 1   Preheat oven to 325 degrees Fahrenheit

Step 2   With an electric mixer, beat cake mix and butter on low for 5 minutes or until it resembles a crumble

Step 3   Reserve 8 ounces and create a crust with the rest by pressing into the bottom of a baking pan (9"x13")

Step 4   Bake for 10 minutes or until edges are just beginning to crisp

Step 5   Remove from heat and cool for 5-10 minutes

Step 6   In a separate bowl, beat cream cheese and frosting with the mixer on medium for 5 minutes or until smooth. Scrape the sides of the bowl as you go.

Step 7   Beat eggs one at a time into the cream cheese and blend for 3 minutes or until smooth

Step 8   Add green food coloring until you reach the desired shade, then beat with a mixer for 2 minutes

Step 9   Beat in crème de menthe for 2 minutes and add more if you prefer a stronger taste

Step 10   Pour cream cheese batter over the crust in the baking pan

Step 11   Top with the 8 ounces of reserved chocolate cake mix crumble

Step 12   Sprinkle the crumble with 1 ounce of chocolate and mint chips

Step 13   Bake for 35 minutes or until set

Step 14   Remove from heat and cool to room temperature

Step 15   Cover the pan with plastic wrap and chill for 2-4 hours

Step 16   Melt the rest of the chocolate and mint chips in a microwaveable bowl and heat in 30 second intervals. Stir after every interval until melted completely.

Step 17   Put chocolate into an icing bag and drizzle chocolate over the cake in any desired pattern

Step 18   Cut into bars before serving

Recipe 17. Vanilla Bean Cheesecake Bars

Preparation time-20 minutes

Servings –16

The List of Ingredients:

Crust

1. 1/8 teaspoon salt
2. 2 ounces confectioners' sugar
3. 1/8 teaspoon cinnamon ground
4. 10 ounces crushed graham crackers
5. 2 ½ ounces butter, melted

Batter

1. 8 ounces granulated sugar
2. 3 eggs
3. 1/2 teaspoon lemon zest
4. 1/3 ounce vanilla extract
5. 1 teaspoon freshly squeezed lemon juice
6. 32 ounces softened cream cheese
7. 2 ounces sour cream

Method:

Step 1   Preheat the oven to 375 degrees Fahrenheit

Step 2   For crust: Mix crumbs, salt, cinnamon, sugar and butter together in a bowl until well combined and press into the bottom of a square baking pan (8"x8") in a single even layer

Step 3   Bake for 10 minutes and remove from the oven, letting it cool while you make the batter

Step 4   With an electric mixer, mix cream cheese and sugar together until smooth and you see peaks forming

Step 5   Beat in eggs, cream, lemon zest and juice, eggs, and vanilla until smooth. Scrape the bowl as you go

Step 6   Spread the batter over the crust in the baking pan

evenly and bake for 40 minutes or until just set in

the center

Step 7   Remove from heat and let the cheesecake cool for

45 minutes. Chill for 1 hour

Recipe 18. Key Lime Pie Cheesecake Bars

Preparation time-20 minutes

Servings –9

The List of Ingredients:

1. ½ teaspoon lime zest

2. 4 ounces Key lime juice

3. 8 ounces refrigerated crescent dinner rolls

4. 14 ounces sweetened condensed milk

5. A pinch of salt

6. 4 ounces softened cream cheese

7. 1egg yolk

8. 8 ounces whipped cream topping

Method:

Step 1   Preheat oven to 375 degrees Fahrenheit

Step 2   Line a baking pan (8"x8") with aluminum foil, letting some foil hang over the edges

Step 3   Lightly coat the foil with cooking spray

Step 4   On a flat surface, unroll the dough and cut into two separate rectangles

Step 5   Roll one piece along the bottom of the baking pan, pressing down to create one solid layer

Step 6   Seal all the seams on the second piece of dough and then cut into 4 strips that are 2" wide each

Step 7   Press the strips of dough along the sides of the baking pan and pinch the area where the dough meets the bottom layer to close

Step 8   Use a fork to pierce the dough gently

Step 9   Bake for 5 minutes

Step 10   Remove from heat and set aside

Step 11   Beat cream cheese, milk, salt, and ½ teaspoon of lime zest in a bowl using an electric mixer until smooth

Step 12   Pour the cream cheesed over the crust in the baking pan and bake for another 20 minutes or until dough on the sides of the pan start to pull away

Step 13   Remove from heat and cool to room temperature

Step 14   Cover the baking pan with aluminum foil and chill for 4 hours

Step 15   Cut cheesecake into bars by using the extra foil on the sides to remove the cake from the pan, then cut bars. Top each one with whipped cream and a sprinkle of the remaining lime zest

Recipe 19. Red Velvet Cheesecake Swirl Brownies

Preparation time-20 minutes

Servings –12

The List of Ingredients:

1. 8 ounces white sugar
2. 4 ounces melted butter, unsalted
3. 1/4 teaspoon of vanilla extract
4. 1 teaspoon distilled white vinegar
5. 2 ounces white sugar

6. 6 ounces all-purpose flour

7. 1/4 teaspoon salt

8. 1 large egg

9. 1 teaspoon vanilla extract

10. 2 slightly beaten eggs

11. 8 ounces softened cream cheese

12. 1 ounce red food coloring

13. 2 ounces cocoa powder, unsweetened

Method:

Step 1   Preheat oven to 350 degrees Fahrenheit

Step 2   Coat a baking pan (8"x8") with cooking spray

Step 3   Whisk butter and 8 ounces of sugar in a bowl, then stir in cocoa, food coloring, 1 teaspoon vanilla, salt and vinegar into the bowl and mix thoroughly after every addition

Step 4   Whisk 2 eggs into the batter until combined thoroughly

Step 5   Slowly add flour to the bowl until just combined

Step 6   Reserve 2 ounces of the batter, and transfer the rest to the baking pan

Step 7   With an electric mixer, beat cream cheese in a separate bowl until fluffy, then add 2 ounces of

sugar, 1 egg and ¼ teaspoon of vanilla into the
cream cheese and blend for 4 minutes or until
smooth

Step 8   Spread the cream cheese over the batter in the
pan so it is smooth on top

Step 9   Drizzle the 2 ounces of cocoa mixture over the
cream cheese and make swirls in the mix by
dragging a skewer through it

Step 10   Bake for 35 mins or when a toothpick can insert
in the middle and come out clean

Step 11   Remove from heat and let the cheesecake bars
cool before slicing and serving

Recipe 20. Strawberry Margarita Cheesecake Bars

Preparation time-20 minutes

Servings –16

The List of Ingredients:

1. 1 teaspoon orange juice
2. 2 ounces sugar
3. 4 ounces strawberry tequila drink mix
4. 8 ounces softened cream cheese
5. ½ ounce tequila

6. 2 room temperature eggs

7. ½ ounce cornstarch

8. 1 teaspoon lime zest

9. 1 package refrigerated sugar cookie dough

10. 1 teaspoon vanilla extract

Method:

Step 1	Preheat oven to 350 degrees Fahrenheit
Step 2	Coat a square baking pan (8"x8") with cooking spray
Step 3	Crumble cookie dough along the bottom of the baking pan and press down to create one even layer that covers the whole surface
Step 4	Bake for 15 minutes, remove from heat and let it cool for 15 minutes
Step 5	Beat cream cheese and sugar in a bowl with an electric mixer until smooth
Step 6	Then add the eggs one at a time to the cream cheese, beating each one into the mixture before adding the next
Step 7	Beat the rest of the ingredients into the mixture until smooth. Scrape the sides of the bowl as you go

Step 8   Pour the cream cheese over the crust in the
            baking pan

Step 9   Bake for 50 minutes or until set

Step 10   Remove from heat and let it cool to room
            temperature then chill for 5 hours

Step 11   Cut into 16 bars before serving

Recipe 21. Caramel Cheesecake Bars

Preparation time-15 minutes

Servings –20

The List of Ingredients:

1.   2 dozen Golden OREO Cookies, divided
2.   ½ ounce water
3.   1 large egg
4.   16 ounces softened cream cheese
5.   7 ounces marshmallow creme
6.   1 ounce melted butter, melted
7.   25 individually wrapped caramel squares

Method:

Step 1   Preheat oven to 350 degrees Fahrenheit

Step 2   Line a 9" baking pan with aluminum foil, leaving enough foil to hang over the edges

Step 3   Coat the foil with cooking spray

Step 4   Place 14 Oreos in a blender until they are a fine crumb consistency

Step 5   Mix the cookie crumbs with butter

Step 6   Form a crust with the mixture from the blender by pressing down on the bottom of a baking pan

Step 7   Bake for 10 minutes, then remove from oven and let the crust cool for 10 minutes

Step 8   Put caramels and water in a microwaveable bowl and cook on high for 30 second intervals or until caramels are melted. Stir after every interval

Step 9   Chop the rest of the cookies into coarse pieces

Step 10   With an electric mixer, beat cream cheese and marshmallow in a large bowl

Step 11   Beat egg into the cream cheese mixture, then stir in the chopped Oreos

Step 12   Pour the cream cheese batter over the crust in the baking pan. Drop the caramel mixture by spoonfuls on the batter and swirl with a skewer

Step 13   Bake for 25 minutes or until set

Step 14   Chill for 4-6 hours

Step 15   Use the excess foil to lift the cheesecake from the

pan and cut

Recipe 22. Toaster Strudel Cheesecake Bars

Preparation time-20 minutes

Servings –18

The List of Ingredients:

1. 12 ounces of graham crackers, crushed for garnish
2. 1/3 ounce vanilla
3. 17 ounces pumpkin butter spread
4. 2 ½ ounces sugar
5. 3 ounces melted white chocolate
6. 2 boxes toaster strudel pumpkin pie pastries

7. 2 large eggs

8. 16 ounces softened cream cheese

Method:

Step 1   Preheat oven to 350 degrees Fahrenheit

Step 2   Coat a baking dish (9"x13") with cooking spray

Step 3   Toast the strudels according to the package **method** and then transfer them to a flat serving dish

Step 4   Beat cream cheese and sugar together using an electric mixer until they are smooth

Step 5   Add vanilla, chocolate and eggs and beat until combined

Step 6   Spread the cream cheese mixture over the toaster strudel and bake Grease 9x13 inch dish with cooking spray.

Step 7   Toast each strudel per method on the box and lay them flat in a baking dish.

Step 8   In a bowl, beat together sugar and cream cheese until smooth.

Step 9   Beat in the white chocolate, vanilla and eggs.

Step 10   Pour in the mixture over Toaster Strudels and stir until smooth using a spatula.

Step 11   Bake for 30 minutes or until set. Remove from
           heat and spread the pumpkin butter over the bars
Step 12   Chill for 2-4 hours

Recipe 23. New York Cheesecake Bars

Preparation time-15 minutes

Servings –24

The List of Ingredients:

1. 35 ounces softened Cream Cheese
2. ½ ounce vanilla
3. 10 ounces crushed graham crackers
4. 1 ½ ounces flour
5. 8 ounces sour cream
6. 18 ¼ ounces cherry pie filling

7. 8 ounces sugar

8. 2 ounces melted butter

9. 4 large eggs

Method:

Step 1   Preheat oven to 325 degrees Fahrenheit

Step 2   Line a baking pan (9"x13") with aluminum foil, leaving extra foil hanging over the edges

Step 3   Mix graham cracker crumbs and melted butter together and create a crust by pressing the crumbs into the bottom of the baking pan in a single layer

Step 4   Using an electric mixer, beat cream cheese, vanilla, sugar and flour together until well combined

Step 5   Mix in sour cream, flour, vanilla and sugar, then add eggs one at a time and blend on low

Step 6   Pour the cream cheese batter over the crust in the baking pan and bake for 45 minutes

Step 7   Remove from heat, let the cheesecake cool completely and then chill for 4-6 hours

Step 8   Pour the pie filling over the cheesecake, use extra foil to remove from the pan and cut into bars before serving

Recipe 24. Peanut Butter and Jelly Cheesecake Bars

Preparation time-15 minutes

Servings –16

The List of Ingredients:

1. 4 ounces strawberry jam

2. 1 ounce butter, melted

3. 8 ounces crushed graham crackers

4. 4 eggs

5. 1 ½ ounces white sugar

6. 1 ½ ounces all-purpose flour

7. 16 ounces softened cream cheese

8. 8 ounces white sugar

9. 4 ounces milk

10. 2 ½ ounce crunchy peanut butter

Method:

Step 1   Preheat oven to 325 degrees Fahrenheit

Step 2   Mix crushed graham crackers, 1 ½ ounces of sugar and butter in a bowl with an electric mixer until well combined

Step 3   Press the graham cracker mixture along the bottom of a springform pan (9") until you have a single even layer for a crust

Step 4   Bake for 10 minutes and remove from heat. Cool the crust while you prepare the cheesecake filling

Step 5   Beat cream cheese, peanut butter, sugar and flour in a large bowl with the mixer until smooth

Step 6   Add eggs one at a time, beating them into the cream cheese after adding each one

Step 7   Blend the milk into the cream cheese mixture and then pour it into the baking pan over the crust

Step 8   Bake for 10 minutes, then reduce heat to 250 degrees Fahrenheit and bake for an additional 40 minutes or until set

Step 9   Remove from heat and let the cheesecake cool to room temperature

Step 10   Chill for 4-6 hours, drizzle jam over the top of the cake in a lattice pattern and the release the springs from the pan, cut into bars and serve

Recipe 25. Cranberry Almond Cheesecake Bars

Preparation time-20 minutes

Servings –16

The List of Ingredients:

Crust

1. 2 ounces melted butter

2. 1 ½ ounces sugar

3. 12 ounces cranberry almond protein granola

Cheesecake Filling

1. 2 eggs
2. 12 ounces cream cheese, low-fat
3. 2 ½ ounces cup sugar
4. 1 ounce all-purpose flour
5. 1teaspoon almond extract
6. 4 ounces Greek plain yogurt

Cranberry Layer

1. 6 ounces canned cranberry sauce, jellied

Topping

1. 2 ½ ounces almonds, sliced

Method:

Step 1   Preheat oven to 350 degrees Fahrenheit

Step 2   Put granola in a blender and pulse until it is ground into a fine meal

Step 3   Transfer the granola to a bowl and add 1 ½ ounces of sugar and butter. Stir until mixture is well-combined

Step 4   Create a crust by pressing the granola down along the bottom of a square baking pan (9"x9") and bake for 8 minutes. Remove from heat and let cool while you make the filling

Step 5   Beat yogurt, cream cheese, flour, sugar, almond and eggs in a large bowl with a mixer until smooth

Step 6   Spread the cheesecake over the crust and drop cranberry sauce over the cheesecake in spoonfuls.

Step 7   Top with sliced almonds and bake for 40 minutes or until set

Step 8   Then remove from heat and let the cheesecake cool to the room temperature then chill for 2-4 hours

Recipe 26. Caramel Pecan Cheesecake Bars

Preparation time-15 minutes

Servings –32

The List of Ingredients:

1. 4 large eggs

2. 8 ounces sour cream

3. ½ ounce water

4. 1 ½ ounces flour

5. 3 ounces baking chocolate, semi-sweet

6. 8 ounces sugar

7. 12 ounces finely crushed Nilla wafers

8. 32 ounces softened cream cheese

9. ½ ounce vanilla

10. 24 individually wrapped caramels

11. 8 ounces chopped pecans, divided

12. 2 ounces melted butter

Method:

Step 1   Heat oven to 325 degrees Fahrenheit.

Step 2   Line a baking pan (9"x13") with aluminum foil,
            leaving extra foil hanging over the edges

Step 3   Reserve 4 ounces of nuts and finely chop the rest
            of the pecans

Step 4   Mix the finely chopped pecans with the wafers
            and butter

Step 5   Create a crust in the bottom of the baking pan by
            pressing the wafer mixture firmly across the
            bottom in a single layer

Step 6   With an electric mixer, beat cream cheese and
            sugar in a bowl until well combined

Step 7   Mix sour cream, vanilla and flour in with the
            cream cheese until smooth. Mix eggs in with the

sour cream by blending on Low speed

Step 8   Pour the cream cheese batter over the crust in the baking pan and bake for 45 minutes or until the middle is just set

Step 9   Let the cheesecake cool to room temperature

Step 10   In a microwaveable bowl, melt caramels and water on high for 1 minutes or until caramels are melted completely. Microwave in 30 second intervals and after every interval.

Step 11   Pour the caramel over the cheesecake and top with the reserved pecans

Step 12   Melt the baking chocolate in the same way as the caramels in the microwave and drizzle over the pecans

Step 13   Chill cheesecake for 4-6 hours and use the extra foil to remove from the pan

Recipe 27. Cranberry Almond Cheesecake Bars

Preparation time-20 minutes

Servings –16

The List of Ingredients:

1. 14 ounces crushed graham crackers
2. 1 1/2 teaspoons almond extract
3. ½ ounce lemon juice
4. cooking spray
5. 16 ounces softened cream cheese

6. 4 ounces melted butter

7. 2 ½ ounces milk, room temperature

8. 2 ounces water

9. 2 ½ ounces almonds, sliced

10. 6 ounces white sugar, divided

11. 6 ounces fresh cranberries

12. 1 ounce white sugar

13. 2 eggs, room temperature

Method:

Step 1   Preheat the oven to 350 degrees Fahrenheit

Step 2   Line a baking dish (9"x13") with foil and coat the foil with cooking spray

Step 3   Using an electric mixer, mix graham crackers, butter and 1 ounce of sugar in a large bowl

Step 4   Create a crust by spreading the graham crackers along the bottom of the pan and pressing down to even it out

Step 5   Bake for 10 minutes, remove from heat and let the crust cool to room temperature

Step 6   Mix cranberries, 2 ounces of sugar and water in a pan on medium high and bring mixture to a boil

Step 7   Cook for 7 minutes or until the cranberries have opened. Remove from heat and cool for 14 minutes

Step 8   Transfer cranberry mixture to a food processor and puree until smooth. If you think the sauce is too thick then you can add water.

Step 9   Mix the rest of the sugar and cream cheese in a bowl with an electric mixer for 5 minutes or until smooth

Step 10   Slowly beat 1 egg at a time into the cream cheese mixture until combined

Step 11   Mix in lemon juice, milk and almond extract on medium low until combined

Step 12   Spread the cream cheese over the crust and add cranberry sauce in small spoonfuls. Use a skewer to create designs in the raspberries

Step 13   Top with almonds and bake for 33 minutes or until set

Step 14   Let the cheesecake cool, the chill it in the refrigerator overnight. Cut in bars before serving

Recipe 28. Simple Cheesecake Bars

Preparation time-10 minutes

Servings –16

The List of Ingredients:

1. 4 ounces sugar

2. 12 ounces crushed graham crackers

3. 2 large eggs

4. ½ teaspoon vanilla

5. 2 ounces melted butter

6. 16 ounces softened cream cheese

Method:

Step 1   Preheat oven to 350 degrees Fahrenheit

Step 2   Combine butter and cookie crumbs together, then create a crust by pressing into the bottom of a 9" baking pan

Step 3   With an electric mixer, beat the cream cheese, sugar and vanilla in a bowl until completely blended

Step 4   Mix eggs into the cream cheese mixture until just combined

Step 5   Pour the batter over the crust in the baking pan

Step 6   Bake for 40 minutes or until set in the center. Remove from heat and cool.

Step 7   Chill overnight, then cut into bars before serving

Recipe 29. Pineapple Cheesecake Bars

Preparation time-30 minutes

Servings –24

The List of Ingredients:

Cheesecake Bars

1. 8 ounce refrigerated crescent dough sheet

2. 16 ounces softened cream cheese

3. 4 ounces granulated sugar

4. 2 large eggs

5. 20 ounces pineapple tidbits in juice,

Brown Sugar Glaze and Toppings

1. 1 teaspoon vanilla

2. 4 ounces heavy whipping cream

3. Whipped topping

4. 24 Maraschino cherries

5. 2 ounces butter

6. 4 ounces brown sugar

Method:

Step 1   Preheat oven to 375 degrees Fahrenheit

Step 2   Coat a baking pan (9"x13") with cooking spray

Step 3   Roll the dough along the bottom of the baking pan and press down to create an even layer

Step 4   Bake for 13 minutes or until just beginning to brown

Step 5   Remove from heat and let the dough cool for 10 minutes

Step 6   Reduce the heat to 325 degrees Fahrenheit

Step 7   Reserve the liquid from the canned pineapple in a bowl

Step 8   With an electric mixer, beat the cream cheese and sugar together until the mixture is smooth. Scrape the side of the bowl as you go.

Step 9   Blend eggs into the mixture 1 at a time, ensuring each one is combined well before blending the next

Step 10   Beat 2 ½ ounces of pineapple juice into the cream cheese with an electric mixer until completely combined

Step 11   Finely chop 4 ounces of pineapple chunks and add to the cream cheese. Stir thoroughly until completely combined

Step 12   Pour the cream cheese mixture over the crust in the baking pan and bake for 30 minutes

Step 13   Remove from the heat and cool the cheesecake for 30 minutes then chill for 2 hours

Step 14   Just before removing bars from the refrigerator, melt butter in a small pan on medium heat Stir in brown sugar and cook for 6 minutes or until the sugar is dissolved completely

Step 15   Reduce heat to low and add vanilla and whipped cream, stirring gently

Step 16   Increase heat to medium and cook for 3 minutes or until the mixture is of desired thickness

Step 17   Remove from the heat and let the pan mixture sit for 30-45 minutes

Step 18   Remove the bars from the fridge and drizzle the
           brown sugar on top before cutting into 24 bars
Step 19   Serve the bars with the rest of the pineapple, then
           a dollop of whipped topping and one cherry

Recipe 30. Eggnog Cheesecake Bars

Preparation time-20 minutes

Servings –16

The List of Ingredients:

Bars

1. 2 ½ ounces eggnog

2. ½ teaspoon cinnamon, ground

3. Salted Caramel

4. 16 ounces refrigerated sugar cookies

5. 8 ounces caramel topping

6. 2 ounces sugar

7. 1 teaspoon coarse sea salt

8. 1egg yolk

9. 8 ounces softened cream cheese

Method:

Step 1   Preheat oven to 350 degrees Fahrenheit

Step 2   Coat a square baking pan (8"x8") with cooking spray

Step 3   Roll half of the cookie dough along the bottom of the baking pan and press down to cover the entire surface

Step 4   Beat cream cheese and eggnog in a bowl with an electric mixer until smooth

Step 5   Beat egg yolk, sugar and ¼ teaspoon of cinnamon into the cream cheese until combined well

Step 6   Pour the cheesecake over the dough in the baking pan

Step 7   Crumble the other half of the cookie dough in a bowl with your fingers and sprinkle over the cream cheese layer in the baking pan

Step 8   Bake for 50 minutes or until set

Step 9   Remove from heat and cool for 45 minutes

Step 10   Chill for 2 hours

Step 11   Put caramel topping in a microwaveable bowl
           and cook on High for 30 seconds. Add salt and
           stir until dissolved

Step 12   Cut the cheesecake into bars and drizzled salted
           caramel over each serving